MW01076724

JUST OUTSIDE
YOUR
Window

Finding Insights, Hope and Joy

Donna Marie Bailey and Charlotte Noyes

Just Outside Your Window
Finding Insights, Hope and Joy

© 2021, Donna Marie Bailey & Charlotte Noyes.

All rights reserved. This book or any portion thereof may not be reproduced or used in any manner whatsoever without the express written permission of the publisher except for the use of brief quotations in a book review.

Print ISBN: 978-1-66780-5-726
eBook ISBN: 978-1-66780-5-733

ACKNOWLEDGMENTS

The Book Sisters – Donna Marie Bailey and Charlotte Noyes – wish to thank the following people who helped with *Just Outside Your Window.*

Cover Design   Bunne Hartmann, Hartmann Design Group

Editorial   Ellen Bond
                    Harry Orenstein

Our thanks to **Anna Kaminska,** guest photographer, for her contributions to this book.

Anna grew up in Poland, where she was involved in underground theater, and influenced by its rich history of pictorial creativity. In addition to art photography, she produces portraits and landscapes in color and black and white, using digital and traditional media. She reflects on the elements that evoke the life of a place or person, transforming reality with the lens in her mind and expressing it through the camera. By carefully paring down the distractions of the larger world, she develops intimacy with the small beauties that surround us, and our shared humanity.

ABOUT THE BOOK SISTERS

The idea for this book began 20 years ago with Charlotte and I cradling our cups of tea and staring at the beautiful mountains of Carmel Valley that were right outside the window. And now, it is with great joy and humility that we offer this book to you, so that in quiet moments you might see things more clearly through the windows of your life. We are honored to be part of your journey.

I learned a long time ago that when a person you trust tells you that they think you need to meet someone, you simply must do it, no matter what. You see, that's how the magic happens. Perhaps the person suggesting the meeting has a feeling that you both share a common story that will make your lives better. I can't begin to guess what it's about, but after many years and occasions when I followed someone's advice and met a new person, my life was changed in some important way. Thank God, I was wise enough to listen.

In 1997, I'd just moved to Carmel, CA and was living in a cozy little garage apartment overlooking Clint Eastwood's Mission Ranch. MFC (My Friend Charlotte as I came to call her), walked in my door and our friendship began. The book you're holding is just one result of the many joys of the sweetest friendship two sisters could ever have.

We bonded immediately over a shared love of great tea! Always black teas with lots of body, yet delicate, and quietly mesmerizing. While poring over grants and piles of data, we sipped our tea, and unapologetically ate more than one slice of Charlotte's homemade bread, slathered with butter. And, like the Brits, any time there was emotional turmoil, these Book Sisters put on the kettle.

In 2007, I moved to the East Coast, leaving my beloved friends, Charlotte *and* California. There are people who are with us no matter where life takes us, and Charlotte and I decided we would stay close with handwritten letters to one another. We'd be like Jane Austen's Bennet sisters...and that's just what happened. Both of us loved writing. We found interesting paper to use or made cards. But neither really cared about the paper. It was opening the envelopes, reading the day-to-day stories of one another's lives and sharing our struggles of parenting, new careers, aging bodies, or sharing the joys of a new book or a movie, and, sometimes, our loss of friends and family.

Some envelopes held pictures, poems, and always a promise we kept...to *write* back very soon. Those letters kept us close. During the long cold winters in the East, they warmed my heart and got me through snowstorms and dreary-sky days.

We shared a dream. One day I'd have the time to write every single day and she'd be outside whenever she wanted, capturing the beauty of the world with her camera. Our children would be grown, we could retire, and begin writing a book that would inspire others and help them slow down and realize the preciousness of life that was always right outside their window. All they had to do was look.

Donna Marie Bailey

*The Book Sisters will donate 20% of the profits
from sales of <u>Just Outside Your Window</u> to
the International Rescue Committee, to support its efforts
in aiding and placing Afghani refugees*

WHAT'S INSIDE

Set wide the window
Let me drink the day

Edith Wharton
Vesalius in Zante

FROM MY WINDOW

I have a third-floor apartment in an old building that isn't in the greatest part of town. But I love the perch that overlooks the most amazing life out there. Life I might never have seen from a nicer apartment in a better part of town.

I've been sitting in corners of rooms in the many homes I've occupied in my nomadic lifetime. I always found the perfect room where the morning light arrived and created a feeling of abundance and reverence when my body says "Get up! You might miss something."

Some mornings I see the fox who seems to violate the rule of being a nocturnal animal, grabbing the early hours just as the sun breaks through the mist that floats down my street. Other mornings, there are doves perched on all three sides of the pitched roof of the church that my living room window frames so perfectly. The "Holy Triumvirate" I call them.

A few weeks ago, a bald eagle sat atop the very unattractive transformer on the telephone pole. Can you believe that? And hawks abound. I'm really going to miss their calls as winter moves in right behind that fog coming down the street.

There are the people...so many stories out my window. They feel like old friends...the man walking his Golden Retriever without ever knowing how happy he makes me feel during this crazy pandemic. People on their bikes heading for work. And the homeless man with his dog who adores him and is well cared for by this man who might just surprise people who believe "*they* shouldn't have an animal unless they can afford to take care of it." Every time *I* see them, *they are taking care of each other*.

The Daisy Scouts constructed a food cabinet that now sits in front of the church. In these times when 1 in 5 of our children is not getting enough to eat, people from every walk of life show up for food and toiletries in the early morning hours or sometimes after dark. I know their stories from my own personal experience as a young child. Watching them open the glass doors, I can still feel my own sadness and shame, and gratitude for the goodness of that Scout troop.

Right outside my window, there's everything life is about. Nature to soothe me. Daily reminders to get up and do something for others, and the gift of inner peace that can be hard to come by these days. I hope you have a place that gives you nourishment and, if not, that you'll begin to create that for yourself.

FATHER FIGURES

He is more than a hero
He is a god in my eyes-
The man who is allowed
To sit beside you – he

Who listens intimately
to the sweet murmur of
your voice…

Sappho

Today is Father's Day. Often, on this holiday, I think that fathers get the short end of the stick. Most of them don't get taken out to a fabulous restaurant. They do the barbecuing. Presents are often "useful" things like a new tool or some golf balls that remind them of all the duffs they experienced on the courses they played. Before we knew tobacco kills us, we'd give them a box of their favorite cigars.

I have such warm memories of my Uncle John's Prince Albert cigars. Sitting on his lap, I'd watch him carefully remove the plastic wrap from the cigar, slide off the band with Albert's picture on it and with the most beautiful smile, he'd slide that paper band onto my ring finger. I felt like a beautiful Princess...so loved by this man.

I was often not with my own Father on his special day. Escaping the drinking and arguing at my house, I spent many of those early days at my grandparents' farm. Uncle John lived right down the road, and I could always count on him to be there for me.

Our experiences with our fathers are so varied. Some of us had nurturing dads. Others of us loved fathers who couldn't love us back the way we needed and deserved. And sadly, some of us suffered violence at the hands of the very man who was supposed to protect us.

No matter our situation with our dads, almost all of us had someone who was a "father-figure" in our lives. Maybe it was a teacher, coach, neighbor, relative, minister, therapist, or even the father of our best friend. He was there, listened to us, took us for ice cream, or planted a garden for us every Spring.

When Father's Day rolls around, or you hear John Mayer sing "Fathers Be Good to Your Daughters," think of someone who loved you and helped you see just how precious you are. Then say ," Happy Father's Day!"

Naomi Shihab Nye Poem

It is difficult to know what to do with so much happiness.
With sadness there is something to rub against,
A wound to tend with lotion and cloth.
When the world falls in around you, you have pieces to pick up,
something to hold in your hands, like ticket stubs or change.

But happiness floats.
It doesn't need you to hold it down.
It doesn't need anything.
Happiness lands on the roof of the next house, singing,
and disappears when it wants to.
You are happy either way.
Even the fact that you once lived in a peaceful tree house
and now live over a quarry of noise and dust
cannot make you unhappy.
Everything has a life of its own,
it too could wake up filled with possibilities
of coffee cake and ripe peaches,
and love even the floor which needs to be swept,
the soiled linens and scratched records...

Since there is no place large enough
to contain so much happiness,
you shrug, you raise your hands, and it flows out of you

into everything you touch. You are not responsible.
You take no credit, as the night sky takes no credit
for the moon, but continues to hold it, and share it,
and in that way, be known.

Naomi Shihab Nye

Loving the In-Between

To be interested in the changing seasons is a happier state of mind than to be hopelessly in love with spring.

-George Santayana

Sometimes, to get from where we are to where we want to be, we have to be willing to be in-between. It can feel like being lost in the woods.

One of the hardest things we have to do as we grow and change is let go of what is old and familiar, what we don't want, and be willing to stand there empty-handed and wait for something new to appear. As human beings with brilliant minds, when standing in the dark we are desperate for meaning, unable to accept that the woods don't have answers.

Being in-between might mean being without work, moving to a city far from our family or deciding whether we truly want children or another love relationship. We ache from it, long for it, need it, deserve it, want it and yet, the time's just not right. We have yet to clear out a place in us so we can receive the next best thing.

Letting go of the familiar is frightening even when people, places, things, and ways of coping have not gotten us even a smidgen closer to what we truly want. Because we think it's less painful to just settle, how can we *ever* get we want and need in our lives?

Our guts churning, we feel a subtle, but persistent restlessness, asking ourselves if it's worth the wait or whether we need to just accept things as they are. The choir in our heads tells us it's "unrealistic," we expect too much, or we're acting like a child and need to just grow up. We all know what being grown up means—giving up the joy that only children are allowed.

The choir members in our head are never our own authentic voices. They are the onion-layered chatter of well-meaning people who contributed to our being lost in the woods in the first place.

So, we stand frozen without answers, directions, or even the sun to guide us out. We can hardly stand it. Yet, we must stand there, surrender, and wait. By surrendering, we make our time in the woods shorter by simply quieting our minds and thanking those voices of fear that in our past kept us safe. Then we stop fighting.

Like falling into a rushing river, the way we stay alive is not by thrashing and gasping for air. We must trust the river to support us, float for a while, finally noticing the beauty of the woods. We breathe in the night sky and trust that when we've made room in our heart and can welcome the unexpected...no longer afraid of letting go of the used-up familiar...the answer will come.

Maria Eugenia Baz Ferreira Poem

To all that is brief and fragile
Superficial, unstable,
To all that lacks foundation
Argument or principles;
To all that is light,
Fleeting, changing, finite
To smoke signals,
Wand roses,
To sea foam
And mists of oblivion...
To all that is light in weight
For itinerants
On this transient earth
Somber raving
With transitory words
And vaporous bubbly wines
I toast
In breakable glasses...

Maria Eugenia Baz Ferreira

LOVE IN THE TIME OF COVID

Now we will feel no rain
for each of us will be shelter for the other.
Now we will feel no cold
for each of us will be warmth for the other.
Now there is no more loneliness
for each of us will be companion to the other.
There is only one life before us
and our seasons will be long and good.

-adapted from an Apache wedding blessing

I have been reading this poem for over 25 years now. Mornings are most often blessed by what I call "my morning books." It's a ritual that brought me through many of life's trying times including divorce, remarriage, and my yearning to find someone who would give me the same kind of comfort I found in this Native blessing.

Today is month 13 of what I call Covid Time. This morning, the Apache blessing was not about romantic love, but about my deep longing and sadness at how separate and isolated I've been since Covid Time began. I'm yearning for a blanket of warm loving friends, gathered together without masks, taking in a collective breath.

This morning I prayed for our world to wake up. I prayed that I might have more time on this Earth to do my part in healing it. Let your heart break open today. Ask what you can do to be "shelter" for another.

MORNING SIMPLICITY

I woke
wanting to write a poem
My heart bubbling over
with words yet unformed

The red chair by the window
that gently calls me every sunrise
asking to hold me and my heart full of words
readies itself

I sit, look out my window
and see the grey wolf
trotting by through the cornfield, stopping to stare at me
And I know, the poem is already written

Donna Bailey

ENDING THE WAR OF REGRETS

Most of us have spent our lives caught up in plans, expectations, ambitions for the future, in regrets, guilt or shame about the past. To come into the present is to stop the war.

Jack Kornfield

My third-floor apartment is not far from the historic center in a quaint Midwestern town. Early mornings I sit in "my little corner" that looks down onto a street having the only incline in this flat Midwestern terrain.

Just before sun up, a man getting his exercise before heading to work ran by, his shoes softly hitting the street, sweat on his shirt. He looked like meditation in motion and my body could feel that runners' high I had until age 45. Sadly, I had to hang up my running shoes. Childbirth and bladder control won out.

Almost immediately however, it dawned on me that I still have my original pain-free knees that take me on walks and hikes for miles and miles...something I wouldn't trade for anything.

I once wrote, *"Regret is a killer of dreams, joy and possibilities. And yet, most of us live our lives looking backward. It happens in small ways and for many it completely blocks the sun."* It's gratitude that helps us remember what really matters.

All the losses—relationships that ended, so many moves, jobs you didn't get, colleges you were unable to afford, times when you dragged yourself past the shame to apply for food stamps because you needed some help—were the gifts that helped you grow, turned fear into adventure, and taught you just how strong and resilient you are.

If you have regrets about something you've given up but might like to do again, like painting, playing a musical instrument, becoming involved in a passionate cause, falling in love again, then what are you waiting for? Pull on that resilience. Give yourself the time you never felt you deserved, stand up to fear, and, by all means, don't wait for those old crazy voices in your head to go away before you "Just Do It!"

ANOTHER BORING DAY

When I was in third grade all I wanted for Christmas that year was a diary. I can't recall if it was because other girls had them, maybe an early awareness of wanting to be a writer? I rarely ever got what I asked for at Christmas. My mother had her own ideas about what girls should have, and it never seemed to include the train set that was on my list every year, nor the chemistry set my neighborhood bestie, Sam, let me play with.

That year, for some reason, my Mom listened, and on Christmas morning under the tree was a white diary with a plastic cover. Etched into it was a cartoonish woman who looked like Dennis the Menace's mother. Above her head read *My Diary*. I was so happy and excited when I opened it and ran right up to my room to put it safely in the drawer of my nightstand.

The next day after school, I ran home, took it from the drawer and realized I couldn't think of anything to say about my day at school. Then, I heard the screen door open. My Daddy was home. Running downstairs to see him staggering across the room, I ran over to him to help him find the sofa. We didn't know the word alcoholic back then—just "a drunk."

In a few minutes the snoring got loud and raspy, I covered him with a bedspread and went back to my room. Opening my diary to that day's empty page, I wrote my first entry "Daddy came home drunk today." The days that followed were carefully accounted for...not with notes about friends, going to movies, who I played with at school, but always about how my Daddy was when he got home, either on his own, dropped off by a friend or delivered by the police.

On the occasional day when he wasn't drunk yet, giving me some sense of a "normal" day, I either didn't have anything to write, or I'd enter "Another boring day."

Many years later I discovered that diary in a box of old photos. I took it out, excited to see what my life had been like in 1956. Leafing through it, I saw some empty pages scattered through the daily pages, but most of them simply described how Daddy was when he got home. Then there were the occasional one-sentence entries — "Nothing happened today," or "Another boring day."

Thank God for every opportunity, awakening, struggle, and therapist that showed me the path to healing and living an incredibly vibrant, interesting, beautiful life...one that I wouldn't change one tiny morsel. My childhood taught me some of the most valuable lessons, but the one I treasure most, is just how precious each day truly is. Even those days that we might say, "Not much happened today." The beautiful sun is there, even when it's raining, and it sets every day with certainty before nature sings us to sleep with its promise to return again tomorrow. Our only job is not to waste one single day, and keep our eyes and hearts open to the preciousness and fragility of our struggling planet, willingly accepting our responsibility to be its stewards.

FINDING SELF-COMPASSION

To see the preciousness of all things, we must bring our full attention to life.

Jack Kornfield

I looked at the full moon last night, realizing how incredibly beautiful she is and wondering why I had missed so many of her wonderful displays over the past year.

Turning off my living room lights, I stood by the window looking at every detail of her face, remembering how, over the years, she'd been my solace during times just like these...periods of painful and exciting transition. Then I felt the tears sting as they rolled across my cheeks. How could I have not noticed her these past months? Apologizing to the moon, suddenly I felt my heart open. Then I could feel the deep compassion for my sweet self.

It has been a hard year. Truth is, life is beautiful, sad, mysterious, and sometimes a downright slog. It never comes in the pretty package we were promised. Our bodies challenge us, we lose faith, the "unexpected" happens, and, for some mysterious reason, we're always surprised at how challenging it is. Just when we think we've got it, feeling like a bird gliding on a thermal, something happens that brings us to our knees.

How do we get to the point in our lives where we find a place of peace and love so that each day, no matter what happens, we know how lucky we are and feel gratitude about another opportunity to see the next full moon.

Don't Underestimate Forgiveness

Everyone says forgiveness is a lovely idea, until they have something to forgive.

C.S. *Lewis*

Though "forgiveness" is one of the most beautiful words ever, it's one of the most challenging actions we ever take in our lives.

When I was twelve years old, my father, the most important person in my world, committed suicide. My world crashed and I thought I would die from the pain. For thirty years I kept him and his memory on a pedestal. I turned my dark grief into anger and blame and built a fortress around my heart to make sure I never felt that pain again.

I blamed his mother for never having loved him, my grandfather for sending a complete stranger to college in place of my father, and my mother for not loving him enough. Most of all, I blamed myself for not doing enough.

Over the years my feelings of anger and self-punishment became more and more solid, creating a wall that extended around my heart and into every aspect of my life. I didn't realize I was in my own prison and couldn't see my own beauty or the joy all around me. I was too busy surviving and protecting myself from what is life's inevitable ups and downs, losses and growth...the beautiful fullness that *is life*.

But I wanted *joy* and *peace*. Hundreds of my daily journals were filled with these two words. It took me years to learn from others what I needed to do so that I could live life in such a way that I swam in it freely and with joy. It took years of work with therapists, healing practitioners, books that fell off shelves, retreats, churches, and some amazing ministers. But most important was my burning intention to find this peaceful place before I died.

Some days I can still feel the sting of my anger and blame. All I need to do now is remember that my attitude never hurts the person I'm blaming. It just takes precious life from *me*.

If you want to be free from the cycle of blaming that is keeping you trapped, the first step… *it will take time*. There is no overnight solution. Always remember to be patient and compassionate with yourself. What you experienced at the hands of someone else was painful and they bear responsibility, but only you can decide to live your life in peace and joy.

So, today—*if you can*—-be open to how your anger and blame keep you trapped. If you long to live outside in the sunshine with the precious time you are given, think about just *starting* your journey…one step at a time.

PERSIAN PRAYER

All that we ought to have
thought and have not thought,
All that we ought to have said,
and have not said,
All that we ought to have done,
and have not done;

All that we ought not to have thought,
and yet have thought,
All that we ought not to have spoken,
and yet have spoken,
All that we ought not to have done,
and yet have done;
For thoughts, words and works,

Pray, we, O God, for forgiveness.

The Whole Cake

Much of my early life—without even recognizing it—I settled for crumbs. Most of the time it showed up in relationships with men who weren't available in so many ways. In all fairness, they wanted love, but didn't have a clue how to get it or give it. They all had stories of fathers who never accepted them, didn't know how to love them, were jealous of them, or fathers who themselves were never loved. Fathers who went to wars and were raised in a culture that told them they weren't men unless they were tough, prideful, and never cried when they fell. How *could* they ever have learned how to love?

I was told by those men, and many others in my life that my needs weren't realistic. That I asked too much, or this was the best I could hope for. So, I became very skilled at settling.

In my mid-forties, I sat in my therapist's office one day telling her all the reasons I stayed with a man who was 14 years my senior, incredibly talented and a misogynist. I loved life with him, wearing little black dresses and getting to know famous people. What woman wouldn't love that? There was only one problem...he was seeing other women. I became good at convincing myself that it was OK. After all, I thought I was pretty lucky to be with him– A woman like me with a man like him? You get the drift.

In my therapist's office one day, she suddenly put her notes down, looked at me and asked, "What's your favorite cake in the world?" I knew that! A yellow cake with whipped cream frosting and sweet strawberries between the layers and on top. A local French bakery had it, I told her.

Often, she gave me assignments when I was leaving. And today, I was to go to Fifi's and buy an entire cake. I was to give none of it away even if I had to throw it in the trash can before

I could finish it. I was to have the whole cake. Then she said, "You deserve the whole cake, Donna. Not the crumbs."

If you 're really unhappy, or settling, and know you aren't getting what you want or need from a relationship or at your job, pay attention to that voice telling you to buy a whole cake for a change. You're worth it! Don't settle for crumbs.

ST PATRICK POEM

I arise today
Through the strength of heaven:
Light of sun,
Radiance of moon,
Splendor of fire,
Speed of lightning,
Swiftness of wind,
Depth of sea,
Stability of earth,
Firmness of rock.

St. Patrick

IS LOVING WORTH IT?

One of my last weekends before moving from my home in California to the Midwest, I spent the afternoon with my 5-year-old granddaughters and their sweet Papa. We began with our ritual...tea with Grammie using real china cups. Gotta raise 'em right!

After a little artwork to tape to my fridge, we headed down to the nearby neighborhood field for our very first family baseball game. As luck would have it, we had the whole field to ourselves!

It only took a few hits, then both of them got that baseball "bug." The feel of smacking a tennis ball with an over-sized bat was addictive, so my son and I got plenty of exercise in the outfield. After a while, the kids were hoarse from screaming with joy and ready to do something else fun!

After some hot chocolate and wiggling their bodies to the rhythm of a street band nearby, we headed back home. Kate hadn't put the bat down, creating stories for its use and appointing herself the "owner" of that bat. Sarah lagged behind, her little lower lip now telling me something was up. Falling back to be with her, I asked her about the lip. "I'm sad because I don't want to go home," she confided. By the time we opened my front door, Kate also had crocodile tears just waiting to roll down her face.

"I'm gonna miss you, Grammie," she volunteered. Almost crying myself, I squatted beside both of them. "Grammie is going to miss you too."

"Do you love me, Grammie?" Katie asked. Struggling to hold back my own tears, I smiled, saying, "Of course I do. More than the moon," Then, this little 5- year- old said something that sums up real love..."I know. When you really love somebody, you really miss them when they're gone."

Part of loving someone is the inevitability of losing them. I say "inevitable" because if we love, we will experience loss...to divorce, death, moving away, unresolved conflicts. And, whether it's our grandchildren, a best friend, or our life partner, the question is whether we eventually can embrace the bittersweet alongside the ecstasy of loving and be open to the joy that love brings even when we know it will hurt.

Not everyone can open their heart again after a loss. I hope you can, knowing that's why we're all here on this planet–*to love and be loved.*

WHEN IS ENOUGH ENOUGH?

I wasn't alone when my eyes opened this morning. Those voices from the past, not even mine in the first place, were already talking away. I was enjoying the highlight of my morning—my fabulous cup of tea. My grin suddenly disappeared, replaced by the frown line that resembled the Wicked Witch in "The Wizard of Oz." That crazy voice couldn't even give me my teatime before she chimed in with "How could you be taking the day off when you have work to do?" Putting my cup back on its saucer, I suddenly felt guilty.

When is enough, enough? What is it in all of us that will not let us rest and just enjoy ourselves fully when it's time to relax and let go?

Thank God I can blame my "dysfunctional family." I spent much of my childhood getting up at 4:00 am, sleeping in a cold farmhouse and never being allowed to just "be." My grandmother's core belief was "Idle hands are the Devil's workshop." We shelled peas if we were going to sit down, ironed clothes if we wanted to watch TV and ALWAYS did our chores, our homework, everyone else's chores and everyone else's homework before we could go out to play. Everything had to be done before there could be any sort of joy or fun. Sound familiar?

Although the United States boasts a high rate of productivity, it's on the backs of American workers who come to work sick with the flu and smear rouge on their cheeks to look good in a meeting. We feel *proud* when we say we haven't taken a single sick day in our careers.

Don't wait for those mule driver voices to get quiet, or for someone else to give you permission to be good to yourself. It just won't happen. You have to begin to say, "I'm taking care of myself because I am SO worth it!" You won't have to leave your partner or your children behind to do it. Just know that putting yourself first is a loving thing to do, not only for you, but those you love.

JUST PULL BACK THE CURTAIN

Lately, thanks to some time under my belt doing meditation, I have been aware of how many times a day—an hour, actually—I think that somehow my life is different or I'm different. When I get up in the morning and don't bound out of bed, pain-free and with the same smooth face and skin I had 20 years ago, I compare myself, and even my aches and pains, to somebody else's.

I look at my bank balance, and think, "How could that possibly be right? By now, I ought to be wading through those bonds, and give a damn that the stock market just dropped 800 points. What in the world did I do wrong to have THIS balance?"

Every time I compare myself to someone else, it leaves me feeling completely alone. It's as if I'm the only one who hurts, doesn't have enough money, hasn't found the love of my life, and can't even drink wine anymore. Later, it really hits me! I start listing every friend and family member I have. Every single one of them has been sick, has parents who are aging, are afraid of a diagnosis, or sad about some loss in their life. They, too, are confused and ashamed about something they "should have done," thinking they "wouldn't be in this predicament," if only—.

My friends aren't unusual or unique. When I pull back the curtain that isolates me and makes me feel ashamed, embarrassed, and believing it must be about me, what I see is the sea of humanity. All of us swimming in the same waters of life.

From now on, when *you* feel alone or find yourself comparing, pull back the curtain. I hope you'll see that we're all swimming and thrashing about in the same ocean.

THE REAL TRUTH ABOUT HAPPINESS

There is almost nothing outside you that can help in any kind of lasting way, unless you are waiting for a donor organ. You can't buy, achieve, or date serenity. Peace of mind is an inside job, unrelated to fame, fortune, or whether your partner loves you.

Anne Lamott

Don't you just hate that? Of all the things life has taught me, I know for absolute certainty that it's just the plain old truth.

It certainly hasn't been for lack of effort. Lord knows, I went to the hardware store looking for bread, and dated men who had "potential," believing that if they would only listen and do what I told them to do, then I'd be happy. I moved from city to city, state to state, not only because I'm a wanderer at heart, but because I was looking for happiness and thinking that a change of scenery could deliver it.

The journey began in my early thirties. Most therapists in the 70s worked with clients on childhood issues. I learned that both my parents did the best they could, but alcoholism and mental health issues meant I had to grow up fast in order to survive in order to take care of my sisters, and later on, my mother. I became a "little adult" at the age of 11.

I was sad and angry then. Why did I have to give up basketball to go to work? Why didn't I get to play and be a pain-in-the-ass teenager? Why did I have to drive my mother to the psychiatrist or stay with her when she was sick and miss school?

The therapist saved my life when she told me the painful truth. "You are never going to have parents who take care of you, Donna. You have to do that for yourself." The bottom dropped out and I angrily turned to her saying, "That's not fair!" "It isn't", she said. "But that's the way it is. You deserved parents who were able to give you all you needed, but I'm sorry to say, only you can give that to yourself now."

Instead of spending a lifetime in anger and resentment, slowly and painfully, I learned and am still learning to accept the truth. Others can add love to my life, but only I can love myself and care for myself in ways that will make me truly happy.

When we look to others, or to things like money, success, or our life partners for our happiness, it's a setup, and will always end in disappointment. Loving ourselves, learning how to care for ourselves, to trust our judgment and develop the courage to go after the things we want in life...that's the only route to true happiness. And, as you learn how, you'll love the feeling of power you have over your own life.

Dawna Markova Poem

They say a child is born
a blank shape to be molded,
a tabula rasa to be written upon.
But children come
like a plant with a rhizome—
its food source,
the genetic coding for what flower it will become,
how often it will bear fruit,
what its artistry is:
all of that born into it with the seed.
The role of the gardener, then,
is simply to discern the manner of plant
or child trying to emerge.
The role of the gardener,
or parent then,
is simply to ask,
"How do I help it grow
into what it is in its roots?"

Dawna Markova

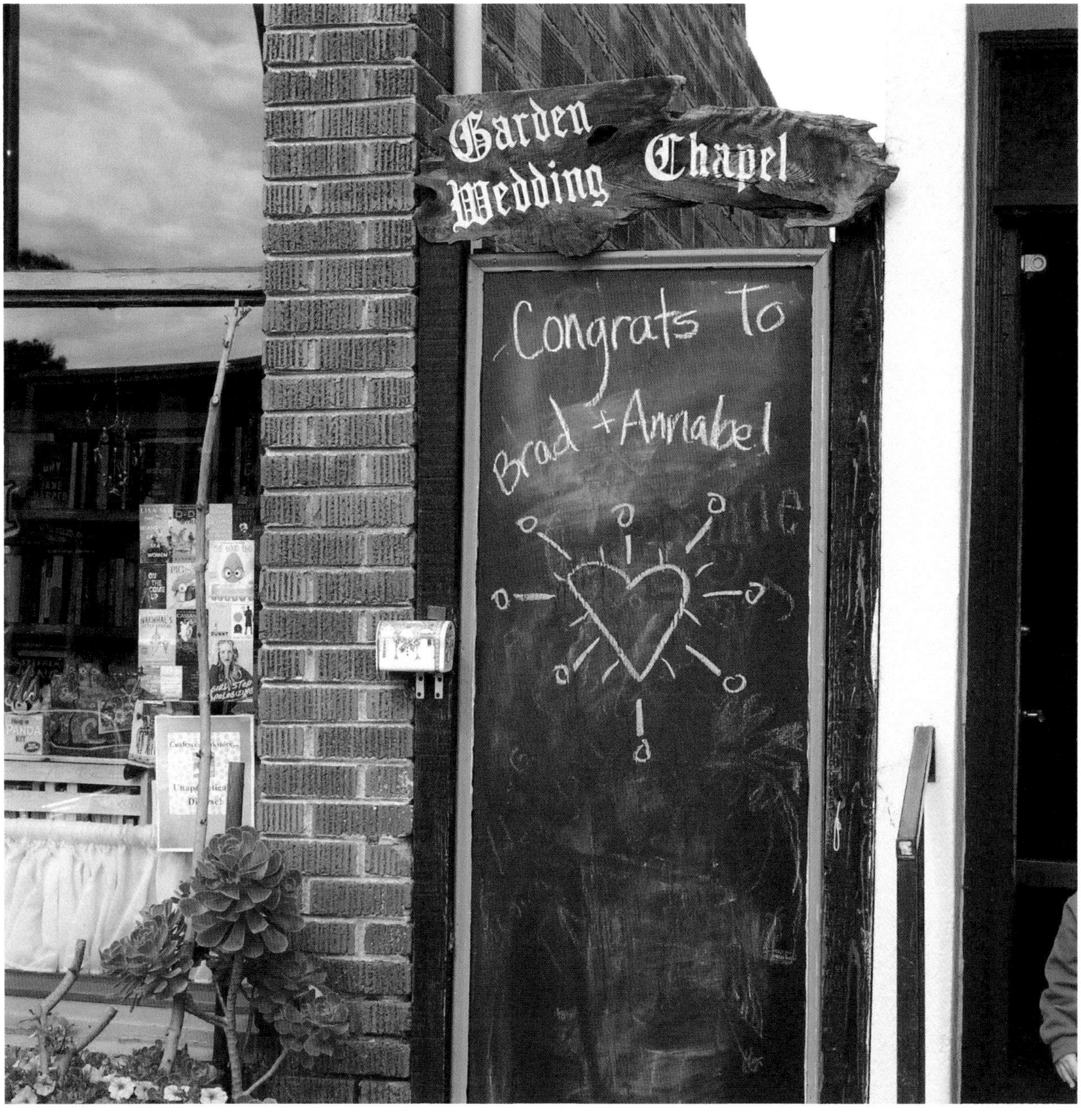
Garden
Wedding
Chapel
Congrats To
Brad + Annabel

Marriage as a Yardstick

I was having lunch with a friend and cheating on my diet bigtime...*ribs* after I'd promised my doctor that I'd only eat seaweed for the next three months if she would wait on recommending a statin.

Hardly breathing while I gobbled those ribs, my friend told me about a couple she knew who had been married for 23 years. In tears, the woman had told her that she was so deeply unhappy in her marriage, confiding, "It died years ago." Looking resigned, the woman had sadly added, "It's OK. I guess that's supposed to happen after 23 years."

My friend looked sad just sharing it with me. Rib bones now piled on my plate, I was feeling the feistiness from red meat. I asked her why, after nine years, she'd never dated anyone after her divorce. Looking around to make sure nobody could hear her, she whispered, "I don't think I can do relationships." Then, even more quietly, she offered her real reason... "I've never told even you this, but I've been married twice." I could feel the deep shame she felt sharing her secret.

I was so sad watching her face --- a face so filled with shame, thinking not only that she had failed at marriage but believing *she* was a failure.

At 59, she'd already given up ever finding love again. All because, like many of us, she used marriage as the yardstick of success.

Our society gives us no other message than those vows in traditional ceremonies, "'til death do us part." And by God, we'd better not leave each other before the Grim Reaper gives us permission!

Using marriage as the measuring stick for success pretty much labels almost all of us failures.

Now, don't get me wrong. When marriage works, and when you find people who are happy after 40 years, still vibrant and in love, it is to be celebrated!

However, by far, most of us will divorce at least once, have a number of short relationships, have a lot of coffee dates, and some will be happily single for some or most of their lives. The Rule of Marriage as the measure of success is no longer valid. It is, however, the gold standard that we're still quite married to.

Every relationship, including marriage, is a success when measured in terms of the fun and beauty, say nothing of the growth we experienced when we were together. Some of us have children born from love, and all of us grew! But we have got to let go of marriage, alone, as our yardstick and release ourselves and others from the labels of success and failure. Anyone who has the courage to pick themselves up, hearts and all, and is willing to risk loving again is always successful.

Thomas Merton Prose

The reality that is present to us and in us:
call it Being...Silence.
And the simple fact that by being attentive, by learning to listen
(or recovering the natural capacity to listen)
we can find ourself engulfed in such happiness that it cannot be explained:
the happiness of being at one with everything in that hidden ground of Love
for which there can be no explanations....

Thomas Merton

THE WONDER OF IT ALL

Oh, but for the wonder that bubbles into my soul...

D.H. Lawrence

When that wonderful Irish doctor walked into my hospital room to deliver, as gently as possible, my cancer diagnosis, it felt not so much like a death sentence, but a big realization that what I would miss most, were I to die, was the *wonder* of life. Right at that moment, I knew I wasn't done with living, and that I would not only survive, but thrive. I would know there was time to gasp and swoon over the beauty of nature, music and my love of minor chords, and the magic of paintings that flowed somehow from artists in ways I can't comprehend.

During the Covid pandemic, Walt Disney saved us when it worked with Pixar to deliver the movie, "Soul." If ever there was a time for an audience, in this year of great suffering the movie confirmed what many of us already knew...our pre-pandemic priorities needed to change...maybe forever.

The most profound moment in that film was when the main character finally opens his eyes, watching a leaf gently fall to the ground. In his life of striving for success, he had missed the most important things...moments like that.

We've had more than a year of isolation from our families and friends. We longed for parks, museums, and restaurants where we feel free to breathe the air again without a mask. Covid has taught us how quickly we can lose our precious lives, and, for the fortunate, we get yet another opportunity to decide how we want to spend each day.

Life is *about* wonder, curiosity, beauty, asking the hard questions and taking action that is good for us, our families and friends, our country, and this irreplaceable planet of ours. It was, after all, three beautiful plants that were used to make the chemo drugs that I hope will give me more time to appreciate the life I never take for granted.

Why Am I So Tired?

Do you ever get to the end of your day feeling like you have been run over by a Mack truck, just to hear this from yourself, "Why am I so tired?" It reads like your Mileage Plus credit card Rewards Program. What did I do to earn this exhaustion?"

Maybe there are a few in the world that *are* lazy, do-nothing folks. You'd think I'd know some of them. But everyone *I* know and see, including the homeless, are doing a great deal— working hard to provide a roof over their heads, care for their children, and feed themselves every day.

We all work very hard, and yet, *very few* of us ever give ourselves the kudos we deserve. We always have that nagging feeling that it's *never enough*.

When I began my consulting career back in the early 80s, I still used a paper calendar with a square for each day. I would enter my appointments, speaking engagements, and the places I had to be on any given day. At the end of the day, I'd always ask myself, "What did I do today?" Then, I'd look at my little square and begin to beat up on myself for "feeling so tired," thinking "I didn't do enough to feel THIS tired."

What wasn't showing up in those squares was how many hours a day I'd spent taking care of my children, packing their lunches, doing laundry, and scrubbing toilets after little boys used them. It was all the stuff I realized I wasn't calling "work" because, like society, I devalued everything that wasn't about earning money. Sound familiar?

Here's what you can do to stop the self-flagellation and judgment that's not only unfair and untrue but makes you downright tired! Instead of making a To-Do list either on paper or in your mind, wait until the end of the day and, before you turn the lights out, make a DONE TODAY list of all the things you did; all the work including seeing family and friends, parenting, household responsibilities, volunteering and helping others, looking for things people in the family can't find...I call this "Uterus as Divining Rod" time. Then, you'll very quickly see what a miracle *you* are and, hopefully, give yourself a big shout-out.

While you're at it, open your calendar and find a space to add some time for putting your feet up, meditating, taking a walk in the woods, reading a mindless novel...you know, the things you only do on vacation. Schedule *one* thing that you love to do each day. Put it on that calendar as if it's *just as* important as everything else. You deserve it!

TO ALL TRAINS

WHEN POSITIVE THINKING IS *NOT* GOOD FOR YOU

I can see the posters...cute little kittens hanging upside down. Words below read, "Hang in There!" And that's supposed to do it for the day. If that fails, there's half a Barnes & Noble full of journals or self-help books just waiting to capture your heart and help you "Just Do It" or "Have a Good Day".

It's a popular thing, this encouragement from authors, athletes wearing Nike, gurus who sell their books, or even supplements using positive thinking as a motivator to action. Often, it's just what we need to get off the sofa and get moving once we've watched too much doom and gloom on our local news station or smartphones.

So, is there anything wrong with this kind of positive thinking? No indeed...*unless we never take steps to change.*

There's something more subtle that we do, called "remembering the good times" that may *not* be positive thinking in the end. We may *feel* that it makes us happy, but what are we doing *day by day* to *keep* creating feelings of happiness? Are we still growing and learning, trying new things, or are we spending our days sitting in our comfy chair or going to the same job that we can't wait to leave when we retire?

Recently, I was talking with my oncologist who was mystified by how well I handled my chemo. "I never see people do this so well and I know they all want to stay alive too. But there's something different about you and I wonder what that is?"

I hadn't really thought about it. It just felt normal to me. But I decided to do what almost always takes me to clarity...I opened my journal and began to write. Eventually the answer came. You see, *I don't want to just stay alive. I want to live. Really* live my days and life with the same curiosity and craving for "more please:" more mornings, sunsets, cute little chipmunks that dart across my feet on the patio and make me laugh out loud at five in the morning. I want to read more of the books in the library, see how the Congress votes on things that matter. I want to live to use my new easel to paint and paint for hours. And, most of all, I want to see what's around the next corner, and watch my kids and their kids grow up. I want more teatimes with my friends and family while I smile watching them fall in love with this ritual that I love so much. That's what living is. It's more than simply staying alive.

As we age, gravity pulls us down. We sit in our lumpy recliners and watch the news. We become more rigid in what foods we eat, are wary of traveling "too far," taking a new course because we don't think we can learn a language anymore. So, our mind begins to look for pleasure in places that are safer. Instead of thinking about what we want to do *now*, we sit and think about what we *have done*. New friends? Nah, it's too late for that. We'll just remember our old ones that have passed. Great memories. You see how it works...

Real living *includes* our memories, and that's wonderful indeed. I have so many great ones I'd never want to forget. But, to live fully, we need to challenge and push ourselves to stay open and find things we've yet to do. Especially those things that we think about over and over and may have wanted to do. Even if they don't make much sense now, we might want to do/try them anyway.

Life is beckoning to be lived as if it's the last day you have. That's true if you're 20, 50 or 90. Next time you sit down in that chair and turn on the TV, remember what my 90-year-old customers told me when they came to my Tea Room: "If you want to stay alive and enjoy life, you gotta keep moving. Don't sit down and never quit learning." I must have listened.

HANG ON TO YOUR BASKETBALL

It's time you realized that you have something in you more powerful and mirac-ulous than the things that affect you and make you dance like a puppet.

Marcus Aurelius

Many years ago, I was struggling in my marriage. I was confused, angry and stuck. A friend told me something that would change my life forever.

"Donna, " she said, "you really need to get your power back." The minute she said that, the image of a basketball came to mind. Perhaps it was because I played basketball in high school and my body still remembered those little "playmakers" who would come out of nowhere and take the ball right out of my hands, leaving me feeling powerless, angry, and embarrassed.

It's easy to lose our basketball. With people at work, our partners and yep, even our own children. In that second when we see someone running down the court with *our* basketball, before we know it, we sink into hopelessness and even despair and shame...our sneakers stuck to the floor with Super Glue. Then, the self-blame and flagellation begin, followed closely by feeling confused and helpless. In short, we feel like a *victim*.

The next time something happens at work, school, in your family or with friends and you feel as if you've been sideswiped, stop and ask yourself if you just gave away your basketball. Revisit what happened and ask if it *really* was your responsibility. If part of it was your problem, then you can make amends and you'll feel as if that basketball is back in your hands. If it wasn't your issue, you can think about how to regain your power. Perhaps you can talk with the person. If that isn't possible because she/he isn't open to a conversation, *when you know your truth*, you'll feel like you have that basketball right in your hands.

If you *often* find yourself feeling powerless, think about talking with someone—perhaps a friend or a professional, who can teach you ways to take control and regain your sense of power.

Your basketball *is* your power, and it belongs to *you*. Without it, you'll feel like a victim.

Setting boundaries, refusing to be with people who sabotage us emotionally, and taking care of ourselves are all healthy ways you can live your life joyfully.

J. M. Barrie Prose

God gave us memory so that we might have roses in December

J. M. Barrie

WHAT TO DO WHEN IT'S JUST TOO MUCH

Back in 1992 I drove across this big old country of ours, leaving a little village in Maine that had been my home for 13 years. The town was idyllic, nestled between a chain of lakes with loons and crystal-clear starry skies at night. Leaving, I thought I'd die from sadness. And oddly, I *felt like I was dying,* from Seasonal Affective Disorder, SAD they call it. I needed light.

I'd like to say within a week I was sipping lattes in a pair of Birkenstocks. After I had been in California for a few weeks, I realized I'd traded lakes for freeways, friends for single-parenting, and my savings were dwindling as I *desperately* looked for work.

Deeply depressed, I knew I couldn't do it alone. So, I went to see a psychiatrist, and left with a prescription for an antidepressant, which I carefully folded up and put in my wallet, knowing I would never use it.

I then found my way to Jenny's office in the trendy, very Berkeley area named after trees. The office was upstairs over the famous Gaia Bookstore. Though I had read almost every self-help book, none of them was doing the trick now.

After inserting slender needles in me from head to toe, my new acupuncturist, Jenny, asked me what was going on in my life. All I could do was cry.

I told her I'd moved from a beautiful little village in Maine to Berkeley and that I was frozen, not from winter, but, instead, from freeways, traffic, noise and the absence of loons, *and* my sweet friends. With a reassuring smile, she told me something I've never forgotten and have used over and over in my life. "When life feels too overwhelming, just make your world smaller. Find a place you love to have coffee each day and just go there. Then, find a park up in the hills with trails you like and just hike those. Go to the same grocery store near your home. Live your life without ever getting on the freeway. Use city streets. Find your places, your people, your favorite sandwich shop and movie theatre. *For now, just make your world very small."*

When in periods of great transition and feeling powerless, hopeless, and fearful, and you don't know how to deal with it all, remember Jenny's words..."Just make your world smaller". It's always made things better for me, and I hope it will for you too.

RUMI POEM

This being human is a guest house.
Every morning a new arrival.

A joy, a depression, a meanness,
Some momentary awareness comes
Of an unexpected visitor.

Welcome and entertain them all!
Even if they are a crowd of sorrows,
Who violently sweep your floor
Empty of its furniture,
Still, treat each guest honorably.
He may be clearing you out
For some new delight.

The dark thought, the shame, the malice.
Meet them at the door laughing and
Invite them in.

Be grateful for whatever comes.
Because each has been sent
As a guide from beyond.

> *Rumi*

DAPHNE ROSE KINGMA PROSE

It is love which fashions us into the fullness of our being-not our looks, not our work, not our wants, not our achievements, not our parents, not our status, not our dreams. These all are the fodder and the filler, the navigating fuels of our lives; but it is love; who we love, how we love, why we love, and that we love which ultimately shapes us.

It is love, before all and after all, in the beginning and in the end that creates us. Today, remembering this, let yourself acknowledge and remember the moments, events and people who bring you, even momentarily, into a true experience of love, and allow the rest, the inescapable mundanities of life, like a cloud, to very quietly drift away.

Daphne Rose Kingma

It's All in the Action

It is easy to sit up and take notice. What is difficult is getting up and taking action.

Honore de Balzac

Many of us spend our lives talking about things we would *like* to do, know we *need* to do, think we *ought* to do, and wish we *could* do. Time goes by and we talk and talk and talk about it, and one day we realize that life is not a dress rehearsal. This time we know that, because our knees need replacing, or we get that dreaded call about our mammogram or, if we're lucky, we just need another Advil to get moving.

I have a good friend who wakes up every morning to a lot of regret about not finishing college, not building a house of his own, not having children, or not learning to play guitar...the list is endless. Like many of us, his childhood wasn't perfect, and he carries the heaviness of that. Perhaps it explains his regret. But when we keep blaming events and people for keeping us from fully living our lives, it's time to take some responsibility. For only when we pull ourselves out of being a victim and take responsibility for our own happiness can we begin to take baby steps toward our dreams by taking action. Picking up the phone and calling a therapist, joining a gym, checking out the guitars and the local music store where they offer lessons, etc.

Beware of the lure of victimhood. It can become comfortable if you aren't careful. Only when you trade it in for taking responsibility in the here and now can you have a *blast* making up for "lost" time! It's never too late to find happiness.

LI PO POEM

The birds have vanished into the sky,
And now the last cloud drains away.

We sit together, the mountain and me,
Until only the mountain remains.

Li Po

Is it Hard to Have Fun?

I was about 34 when I finally went to a therapist. As is true for most of us, I had finally realized that when I looked at problems I was having in my life and my marriage, *I* was the common denominator.

Recalling an incident from the night before I knew that, for once at least, my husband was right. I was complaining about all the things he hadn't done, or hadn't done *right*. Ordinarily, he just walked away when I did that. But this time, he put his hands on his hips and said, "Donna, if I did 100 things right today, you'd find the one thing I did wrong." That was the moment my dime dropped, and I knew I needed help.

I arrived right on time, dressed to the nines despite the blizzard. Judy poured me a cup of tea and asked how I was doing? I went right to problems at work and after I took a breath, she asked me, "Donna, you said you have Thursday off this week, right?" "Yes," I replied. "So, what are you going to do for fun?" she asked.

She may as well have been speaking Italian. I was frozen in place, unable to answer. Smart lady that she was, she continued, "You know there's a great exhibit at Bates College. You'd enjoy that." I said, "It's too far to drive to Auburn." "OK, how about you go spend some time in Barnes & Noble and get yourself a good book?" Yes, I thought. I can do that. But she hadn't finished. "The only thing is, I don't want you to look in the Self-Help section or the Psychology section. How about a good novel?" Blank stare was all I had. Realizing I needed more direction on my homework, she added, "I want you to buy Tom Robbins' *Jitterbug Perfume*. It's funny and I bet you'll love it."

Now, I can *do* assignments! So, I did exactly as I was told, and took that book home and began to read, and even laugh. What I suddenly realized was that I hadn't read anything for fun since I was a child. My life had gotten serious fast. And, in fact, the ideas for what "fun" was had been pretty non-existent. I had very few memories of laughing as a child and my family photos confirmed it.

This is how I realized fun was missing in my life. Having to grow up too early meant no time for that. And, even when I was at my Grandmother's, there was never fun until all the chores were done. Most days, that was after dark.

Six months after that therapy session, I was laughing again and reading more Tom Robbins. So, I bought my family tickets to New York City. After the Macy's Thanksgiving Day Parade, we headed for Macy's to stand in line to see that fabulous Santa. Even then, I knew the trip wasn't only for my son. *My kid needed it too.*

Find the fun in *your* life, and maybe you'll discover it's never too late to learn.

ANNEMAREE ROWLEY POEM AND MEDITATION

Sometimes I am not sure of the steps to take and I falter on the tightrope of indecision
Sometimes I simply walk straight ahead without a hint of hesitation
Sometimes I want to hide beneath the covers and not face the world today
Sometimes I bounce out of my bed with a spring in my step...ready to play
Sometimes I can barely lift my feet
Sometimes I can't stop dancing

For I am...only human. For I am...only human

Sometimes I don't want to speak
Sometimes I want to shout to the skies
Sometimes I am brazen
Sometimes I am shy
Sometimes I don't like listening
And sometimes I hear so clearly

Sometimes simplicity is the key
Sometimes complexity is the norm
Sometimes I feel trapped
Sometimes I feel free
Sometimes the sun is shining
Sometimes darkness envelops me

Sometimes I truly know
Sometimes I doubt completely
Sometimes I am stuck
Sometimes I flow

Sometimes I feel the warmth on my skin
Sometimes the wind chills my bones

Sometimes I feel pretty
Sometimes I feel plain
Sometimes I am so wise
Sometimes so foolish
Sometimes I know where I am going
Sometimes I have lost my way.

For...I am only human

Sometimes I can give you my time
Sometimes I need that time for me
Sometimes I reach for the stars
Sometimes I dig deep into the sand
Sometimes I push you away
Sometimes I hold you in my arms

Sometimes things cannot be fixed
No matter how hard I try
They break and shatter and fall off the wall
And so I just want to cry

For I am...only human

Sometimes my heart swells
Sometimes it closes down
Sometimes I show my vulnerability

Sometimes I hide away
Sometimes I am so strong
Sometimes I am so frail
Sometimes I have wanted to die
Sometimes I see no wrong

And sometimes...sometimes...little fright bubbles make me shiver
and I realize I have been too frightened to let them show...
And then I reflect and know....

As the sages have said...and ancient texts prescribe
Sometimes life is simply a balance between holding on....and letting go

For do we not all feel the same..............sometimes?

Annemaree Rowley

GERARD MANLEY HOPKINS POEM

Glory be to God for dappled things--
    For skies of couple-color as a brindled cow;
    For rose-moles all in stipple
        upon trout that swim;
Fresh-firecoal chestnut-falls; finches' wings;
    Landscape plotted and pieced--fold, fallow,
        and plough;
    And all trades, their gear and tackle
        and trim.

All things counter, original, spare, strange;
    Whatever is fickle, freckled
        (who knows how?)
    With swift, slow; sweet, sour; adazzle, dim;
He fathers forth--whose beauty is past change:
    Praise him

    Gerard Manley Hopkins

My Best Valentine's Day Gift

This was originally a blog I wrote for Donna's Big Red Chair. I am including it in this book because it was far and away everyone's favorite. I hope you will find it helpful in your life as well.

FTD must have been the original St. Valentine, or the Saint was a hell of an entrepreneur. Roses are synonymous with LOVE. Thanks to the media, not a man or woman alive escapes the message that "your sweetheart will give you *anything* if you remember the roses." And, according to Valentine's Day rules, the roses in buckets at the local grocer do not count.

Many years ago, I certainly believed my husband *knew* that, but just in case he didn't, as we strolled by a downtown florist I "oohed" and "aahed" over those roses in the window. Now I was *sure* he got the message.

Enter V Day in rural Maine. The year was 1983. It was the same year we purchased our first desktop computer and Dell became a household word. I was like a kid playing in the mud. As a burgeoning writer, I loved that computer! The idea of never buying carbon paper again was almost orgasmic.

I woke up that morning to the second day of a Nor'easter. The lake was frozen solid, the roads plowed during the night were now piling up with snow again. My first thought was that the FTD guy would make it. It just might be later. And the titillating wait began.

My husband was already outside with the snowblower, and without even so much as a "Happy Valentine's Day, Sweetheart", I saw him jump in his car and head for work. A bit tweaked, I thought, "It's OK. He just wants to surprise me when the roses come." But not only were there no FTD trucks on the road that day, even the snowplows had trouble staying on the road.

Darkness came early to Maine in February, but I didn't give up hope. I had put on my little black dress, made lasagna for dinner and I bought a pricey wine.

About 5 o'clock the door opened, and my husband came in, brushing off the snow. "What's for dinner?" he asked. WHAT???!!! OK. I saw the big bag and knew the roses were in there in that crystal vase I saw on TV.

"Happy Valentine's Day!". He smiled and handed me the bag. It felt so *light*. Slowly reaching into the bag, my heart dropped, as I pulled out a book. I was surprised, angry, and very disappointed. The words came rolling off my tongue, "You got me a *book* for Valentine's? Are you kidding?" I saw his face fall as if it had lost all signs of life.

As he walked away, I felt so ashamed and yet still filled with disappointment and anger. How could he not *know* I wanted roses? Remembering the walk by the florist, I thought—any man with a *brain* should know his sweetheart wants roses.

After what seemed like hours, my husband reappeared and we sat down to cold lasagna, half a candle, and a Golden Retriever who had retreated under the table. "Donna", he said, "do you know what I went through to get you that book? I wanted you to enjoy the computer because I know how important it is to you. I drove in a blizzard all the way to Boston (almost 200 miles) to get this book. I thought you would appreciate it, but I can see you don't."

My heart sank. I knew that all the apologies in the world couldn't make up for the words that I could never take back.

That day my life changed in ways that were profound and permanent. For the first time I knew that men want to make us happy. That they have their own ways of showing love. That they can't read our minds. Our expectations of them are based not on their world, but on *our* preconceived notions of what love looks like. That Valentine's Day, love came from Barnes

& Noble, not from FTD. It came with such beautiful intention and thought. All I had to do was to be open to what *he* called love.

That Valentine's Day was the best one ever. It changed me in so many ways. Though I'm still in love with roses, I've learned that I can give those to myself. Even red roses pale when I think of the things a sweet relationship brings to me.

Why I Didn't Like my Journal

About four months ago, before Covid changed everything, I actually went inside a Marshall's. Not everyone pronounces that right...for seasoned "Sport Shoppers" such as myself, we call it, "Mar Shaaaaaaals". It's as close as most of us will ever get to Rodeo Drive.

I bought a beautiful journal, having recently been inspired by a podcast. The podcast's message was to journal all our positive thoughts we had in the mornings. The days came and went, but I just couldn't make myself begin writing in that journal. Maybe it was "Journal Block," rather than my best friend, "Writer's Block?"

One day it hit me. I couldn't, or wouldn't, write in it until I felt positive about life. As my mother used to say, "If you can't say anything nice, don't say anything at all." I guess my first thoughts in the morning weren't always positive...what was wrong with me?

The answer is a resounding NOTHING. Nothing was wrong with me, but something was very wrong with the voice in my head that told me I should feel happy in the morning...not *some* mornings, but *every* morning. The voices don't have much patience for anything else but perfection...and that means, *be happy*...always.

We come into this world with *all* our feelings and there's a time and place for all of them. Yes, *anger* too. We need every single one of them. It's just that we've learned that some, like *happiness*, are good, and *anger and sadness*, not so good.

Unless we find a way to befriend and even love them all, we can never live life fully. You can't have an authentic life without each and every one of those feelings. Open up and invite *all* your feelings in. Allow them to guide you through the ups and downs of a life well-lived. Each one of them has healing to offer if you only see them as *friends*.

PUEBLO VERSE

Hold on to what is good
    even if it is a handful of earth.
Hold on to what you believe
    even if it is a tree which stands by itself.
Hold on to what you must do
    even if it a long way from here.
Hold on to life
    even when it is easier letting go.
Hold on to my hand
    even when I have gone away from you.

Pueblo verse

Spending Your Holidays with Martha or Joy?

Don't get me wrong. I LOVE LOVE LOVE holidays. I'm Irish and I look for any reason to celebrate. But when I follow the Martha Stewart hand-cut breadcrumb trail, it can lead me right to the Witch's cottage.

When I was a child, let's just say my family had "issues." To be fair, they were pretty big issues. So, as a child, I created a fantasy family where things were safe, predictable, and did I say perfect? I promised myself that when I grew up and had my own children, our holidays were going to be just like the movies!

Halloween meant the perfect costumes, orange and black food, baked cupcakes for all the kids in their classes, house decorations...the works! Thanksgiving was defined by a perky, perfectly cooked bird that entered the oven at 4 a.m. whether I was nursing my second child or not. The table was so full it could have fed the masses, and, of course, a full breakfast of homemade (not Bisquick!) pancakes with blueberries, long out of season and running $15.00 a pint. And Christmas...well, you get the picture. But in it, be sure to include a handmade gingerbread house that cost me $50.00. So, the kids couldn't touch it, much less eat it.

Fantasy was my reality. I had no idea until much later in life that my kids could have cared less. All they wanted was to enjoy the holidays. And as for my husband, the only thing he cared about was not missing the big game!

It was all for me, really. All those holidays. I needed them. The child inside of me needed them. And well into my 40s, my child was driving the car. Bless her sweet little heart.

I wish I could tell you I grew up and now never experience unrealistic expectations about holidays. But it's not an easy thing to recover from. I'm not there yet. I still want what I want sometimes. But I catch myself most of the time and feel better when I remember that we are only on the earth for a short time, and *that* time should be spent loving, growing, and filled to the brim with gratitude.

None of us is without expectations and needs when it comes to holidays. The key, however, is to not let Martha set you up to believe that it's about the perfect tree, costume, turkey stuffing, or the gingerbread house. Truth is, the holidays are about how it feels to love your very imperfect self so that you can bring the joy of any kind of holiday experience to those who—trust me—care less about the turkey than being with you.

LISTEN TO YOUR HEART

Today I had the joy of spending the afternoon with my twin granddaughters. They are one of life's greatest joys and having them makes me feel so alive. Not *so* alive that one of them didn't think I needed to have my heart checked out. With her stethoscope in those sweet little ears, Kate placed the disc over my heart, listening intently. Trying to be funny, I quoted the Grinch, "Do you think my heart is 'two sizes too small'?" I asked her. Without even looking up, I heard this precious little voice say, "No, Grammie. Your heart is just perfect."

It brought tears to my eyes. How many times in my life I longed to hear that my heart and my sweet self were just perfect the way they were. Maybe you've felt that way too?

Perhaps our parents couldn't say that. There may have been teachers who couldn't see just how perfect we were, despite our struggle to understand algebra, or paint a bulletin board-worthy snowman. And somewhere along the way, we may have had a partner who wanted us to be someone we weren't. Maybe we've spent too much of our lives trying to be someone other than ourselves, feeling that nobody could ever love us if they knew who we "really were." Feeling somehow as if we were imposters.

But, *Dr. Kate* had it right! *My* heart, *your* heart, are just *perfect*. You are perfect in every way. Does that mean we don't make mistakes or need to grow in certain areas? Maybe we've done things, said things that we regret. But that is something we *did*. Not who we *are*. The essential *you,* however, is just as perfect as the day you were born.

Does someone you know need to hear that their heart is just fine? Maybe you can let them know that the next time you are listening to them *without your stethoscope...*with just your loving attention.

Victor Hugo Poem

Be like the bird, who
Pausing in his flight
On limb too slight
Feels it give way beneath him
Yet sings
Knowing he has wings.

Victor Hugo

Do You Think I'm Being Selfish?

That is the ever-present question for us, even when we aren't aware of it. And the decisions we make when the "voice" creeps in or lambasts us, destroying any self-confidence we might have had, are made as quickly as that reflex that happens when the doctor taps your knee with the little rubber hammer. And for girls and women, this self-doubt is even more powerful.

I was diagnosed with cancer last fall. A serious kind that sometimes throws many people into a state of resignation. But, for some reason beyond even my understanding, my reaction was relatively calm. Looking at my sweet, sad-looking doctor, I said, "O.K. but I don't think it's my time yet. I have some things I have to do here." I've held on to that deep belief and faith. Of course, there are moments, hours, and sometimes a whole day when I am in the weeds.

To heal, I've needed to keep the focus on myself, including reducing stress. Stress hormones kill good cells, while those amazing hormones of relaxation, happiness, and feeling empowered nurture you and your cells. My plan was to heal and to enjoy each day. In order to do that I had to make choices every single day that would help me do the healing. It often meant eliminating things like Ben and Jerry's, and an occasional glass of Chardonnay, and being more selective about who could be my supporters and cheerleaders in this healing journey ahead. I pulled in, got clear and sometimes fierce about staying as much as possible, in a positive environment. This safe, nurturing place was called my "cocoon."

Cancer is a full-time job. To handle it, much less heal from it, *requires* focusing on one's health and healing. Making nutritious foods, when some days it's all you can do to make a cup of tea; relying on friends, family, and people from local organizations like wellness centers to deliver it. Endless trips for lab work, treatments, doctors' appointments. Sleeping, napping, catching up on the sleep you lose from treatments, and trying to find a day to spend with your grandchildren or talk with a friend when you are at your "best."

There were times, like saying "No" to my kids about keeping my grandson or telling my sweet partner he needed to go home when I was overstimulated or too cranky to be with anybody, or simply needed my alone time. I had to continue to learn how to speak up during chemo when I needed something I wasn't getting. And, even learning to accept, gracefully, the kindness of people from organizations that delivered fresh healthy foods prepared not only for me, but for my caregivers, was challenging for me. I heard the voices that live in my head questioning my worth, telling me I should be able to do it myself. Voices telling me it was *mean* to send my sweet partner home. That feeling sorry for myself when others "had it a lot worse than I did," was just being selfish. Do you ever hear voices like that?

Do you think I was being selfish or self-centered? And when *you* are sick, do you sometimes hear those voices? How about when you aren't sick and just need something? Some peace and quiet, a new outfit, time to go for a walk alone, a latte from Starbucks instead of making it yourself? I'm just going to say it, and hope you'll do some work to be able to arrive at this place one day soon. It's about staying healthy, having a long joyful life, being a good partner or parent...and most of all *it's* the *right* thing to do.

You are not selfish to want or have the things I mentioned above or fill in your own wants here _____; it's self-love—a human need. And you *so* deserve it.

Self-caring and asking for what you want, and need won't end your marriage, make you a bad parent, or cause someone who really loves you and wants the best for you to leave you. You are deserving. Don't listen to the voices in your head that tell you otherwise. Smile kindly and tell them to take a *long* vacation. Treat yourself the same way you would treat your best friend. And...enjoy!

HOW I LEARNED TO SURRENDER

For some of us, receiving can be really hard. It makes us squirmy, uncomfortable, and sometimes even fearful. *My* biggest lesson about receiving came one snowy Christmas when I was literally brought to my knees.

My husband came home from work one late winter afternoon and barely said "Hello." Watching him squat down to put on his running shoes, I felt ignored. I'd been home all day nursing our 5-month-old son, cleaning the house for the upcoming holidays, and desperately trying—without success—to nap.

"Hold on Mister! It's *me* that's going for the run!" I screeched, quite forgetting the fact that dark was approaching, and I couldn't see squat after dusk. Little Miss Stubborn darted out the door heading anywhere but toward children. Did I mention we lived in Maine and that "White Christmas" was already on the roads?

The next thing I knew I was lying in a pothole, my legs bleeding, and I was unable to walk. Leave it to me! Angry and feeling indigestion from the crow I was eating, I hobbled home on what I was later to learn was a broken foot. I protested, "It's not broken!" all the way to the hospital ER. I was shocked when the X-ray machine disagreed. I headed home with a cast up to the knee and a pair of crutches. What the ER failed to give me was a personal shopper and a nanny. I hadn't shopped for one single present.

For the first time in my life, I was down for the count. This time, I was unable to pull off my usual Martha Stewart Christmas. In fact, I couldn't even carry my baby upstairs by myself. News flash! *I had to ask for help.*

What makes it so difficult for some of us to receive...to ask for help? Some would say for men it's always been a "sign of weakness," a crazy message we often give little boys. And for women, self-sufficiency is highly valued. Our dinosaur brain is still wired to focus on the needs of others even if we can't *walk to them.*

Some of us are afraid to be vulnerable. If we had parents who weren't able to take care of us, or had a single mom who was too overwhelmed, we had to do it on our own in order to survive. Self-reliance wasn't a choice. It was a necessity.

That Christmas was life changing. Forced to let go and ask for help, I found out that people would be there for me *and* that they were so happy when I asked them to go shopping for presents and groceries or take care of the baby while I got a shower.

I was moved to tears when, without asking, my women friends came over with food, brought me my favorite tea, and took care of everything without my uttering a word. It felt wonderful. I felt so safe and loved. I realized that not only did it feel wonderful for *me,* but everyone helping me felt the same joy.

Give someone a gift by asking them to help you the next time you feel overwhelmed and need a hand. And when the tables are turned, *reciprocate.* Then, you can feel the joy that giving brings.

HENRY JAMES PROSE

There are few hours in life more agreeable than the hour devoted to the ceremony known as afternoon tea.

Henry James

September Blessing

Falling into happiness
floating like cotton candy,
landing on a spider's web.
So dependable.

I open my arms wide,
rise up on my toes.
Pink lemonade nails catching the sun,
I push off.

Almost giddy!
I want this.

She gave me the good news.
From nowhere
they rose from my heart...

jerking sobs,
as if they would stay forever.

Empty of meaning.
Confused, wretched...
my face smiling
asking, "Why can't you stay?"

Happiness appears like a child
playing hide-and-seek.

In a flash, wizard-wand,
leaving only mystery,

Returning,
It asks to rest in my heart.
Trusting that spider's web,
smiling...I surrendered

Donna Bailey, September 28, 2021

Early in the morning, five days ago, my sweetheart and I were about to leave a gorgeous lakeside retreat where we'd spent a week just getting away from the stress of the past year.

A year of my cancer diagnosis and treatment and so much fear and uncertainty...no matter how *well* we both did it together.

It was so still and beautiful on the lake, trees ablaze with fall colors. White birches hanging over the water brought memories of Maine.

Breaking the stillness, suddenly my phone rang. Looking down, I saw it was my doctor's office. Having made a commitment to deal with "reality"—one being the results of my PET scan— when I got home, I decided not to answer. But a voice said it was time to put on my big girl pants and take the call. I make it a practice to listen when *that particular wise voice* directs. Lifting the phone to my ear, I heard my doctor's wonderful nurse simply say, "Donna, we got your test results back and there's no sign of cancer anywhere in your body." Shocked, all I could utter was "Thank you." Then, I just hung up and began to sob.

I've spent the last year with the deep belief that I wasn't going to die *just yet.* As I calmly and confidently said to my oncologist when he delivered the news about the prognosis for pancreatic cancer " I don't think it's my time. I still have work to do here." But on *that* morning, when my phone rang, I was *terrified.*

"Fear and joy often ride the same horse.", I've always said. We all have fears of feeling the joy of happiness.

"What if it's bad news? I need to *prepare myself for it."* Believing, of course, that if we don't hope *too much,* or feel *too happy,* it won't hurt as much. Maybe it's the way our brain thinks it's helping to protect us?. I don't have the answer to that. But I do know that from now on, I'm going to be more aware when it happens. *Living in fear for any reason takes my precious time.* Time I'd rather use *to feel the all-out beauty of JOY!*

I hope you'll be aware the next time you feel giddy and start to hit your mute button. Let yourself *feel it all,* my friends.

LAO TZE POEM

Always we hope
someone else has the answer.
Some other place will be better,
some other time
it will all turn out.

This is it,
No one else has the answer.
No other place will be better,
and it has already turned out.

At the center of your being you have the answer;
you know who you are and you know what you want.

There is no need
to run outside
for better seeing.

Nor to peer from a window.

Rather abide at
the center of your being;
for the more you leave it
the less you learn.

Search your heart
and see
the way to do
is to be.

Lao Tze (attributed)

LIST OF SOURCES

<u>Poetry</u>

Sappho, public domain

Naomi Shihab Nye, "So Much Happiness" *Everything Comes Next: Collected and New Poems,* In press, Green Willow/Harper Collins, by permission

Maria Eugenia Baz Ferreira, "Vaso Furtvo" (Quick Drink)*, Earth Prayers*, public domain

Apache Wedding Blessing, public domain

C.S. Lewis, public domain

Edith Wharton, *Vesalius in Zante*, 1902, public domain

St. Patrick (attribution), "Morning Prayer" 1st stanza, St. Patrick Breastplate, public domain

Marcus Aurelius, public domain

Rumi (Jalāl ad-Dīn Muhammad Rūmī), *The Guest House*, public domain

Dawna Markova Poem, by permission of the author

Honore de Balzac, public domain

Li Po, public domain

Gerard Manley Hopkins, "Pied Beauty," public domain

Pueblo Verse, public domain

Victor Hugo, "The Church of" last verse, *Songs of Dusk,* public domain

Lao Tze, *(attribution) A Grateful Heart: Daily Blessings for the Evening meal from Buddha to the Beatles*, M.J. Ryan, 1994, public domain

Prose

George Santayana, "Season, Change, Spring, Love," public domain

Jack Kornfield, by permission of the author

Anne Lamott, *Almost Everything: Notes on Hope*, Riverhead Books, 2018, by permission of the author

Thomas Merton, from letter to Amiga Chakravarty, in the *Hidden Ground of Love, 1985,* By permission of Thomas Merton Center, Bellarmine University.

D.H. Lawrence, *Song of a Man Who Has Come Through,* public domain

J.M. Barrie, *A Window in Thrums,* public domain

Daphne Rose Kingma, *365 Days of Love (Dec 29),* by permission of the author

Henry James, public domain

Internet Sources

Annemaree Rowley, *Sometimes*, coolcalmandcollected.com.au, Yoga, Meditation, Tours & Retreats, by permission of author

Photography

Anna Kaminska, www.akaminska.com Space, p. 51, Mars, p. 105, Moon, p. 109

Louisa Pike Noyes, p. 5

F. Leigh Noyes, p. 87